HOW PROJECTS ARE RUN

Shoot the Project Manager

Ebenezer Adjei

meerdom@ditec.com.au

Version 1.0

August 2019

DISCLAIMER AND TERMS OF USE

DEDICATION

I am dedicating this book to Daavi.

You made me and you will always be part of me. Thank you. Laryea.

SUBSCRIPTION

Please subscribe to the email list using meerdom@ditec.com.au

EMAIL WITH REQUEST TO REPORT TYPOS AND ERRORS

Please email your request about typo and errors to
meerdom@ditec.com.au

v

Table of Content

CHAPTER ONE
WELCOME

This is a short story from *The Plain of Plenty*. It is called *How projects are run. Shoot the project manager!* Here mobs of meerkats lived happily until about ten seasons ago when their quiet existence was shattered by predators, mainly a clan of hyenas, The Sharp Teeth Gang.

The *Sharp Teeth Gang* decimated the meerkat population. To neutralize the *Sharp Teeth Gang*, the meerkat settled on building fortifications to the tunnels. As luck will have it, they decided to appoint a project manager to build the fortifications. *Kiikidee* was the project manager and the meerkats went through five stages of emotions in the delivery of the project.

The five stages of emotions:
1. Excitement - This is at the start of the project when the project team is all about preparation and setting the project on a solid footing
2. Confusion and worry - when finding your way through a project seemed unending.
3. Getting wrongdoers - you have been working on the project for a while. Then some events come up that seems to have been deliberately put in your way.
4. Just persecute anyone - sometimes you feel any persecution

will satisfy the project team. You have worked so hard, yet the end seems so far away... sometimes you shoot the project manager

5. Adornment of the observers - now the project has been delivered, and as we know, success has many parents. Here we reward those that are left standing. All observers!

Then everyone went home.

CHAPTER TWO

WHAT IS PROJECT MANAGEMENT ANYWAY?

Project Management is both an art and a science. It is an art in that you have to work with people to bring the best out of them. You have to tease out of them the best outputs when sometimes they are not even sure they have it. It is an art of turning people to perform at the highest levels.

Besides, project management is a science. The techniques, methodologies and others you employ to manage and push the project matter. It is the combination of these that make the project manager who he or she is. How much of it is science and how much of it is art is up for debate. The most important at the moment is to see that the project is implemented and the benefits realised!

Projects regularly happen because a senior member of the group has recognised a problem brewing that needs attention. He had either been observing the problem develop and has been waiting for the opportune time to address it. Many a time, he had picked the concept up from a forum like a conference with peers. He thought it was a good idea for his organisation to pursue. Or it could be someone else's idea. Whatever it was, the problem was noticed and was addressed before it was too late.

A project is an activity that falls outside what is considered 'normal' operations. Project management is the how we bring people, resources, methodologies, tools and measures together to produce that activity. The magic is the flair with which the project manager applies his trade.

INTRODUCTION

Meerdom was a collection of colonies of meerkats in the *Plain of Plenty*. They lived their lives well past their teens here. Towards the end of their lives, they either died of old age or sickness. Sometimes they were taken by the predators that continually preyed on their communities.

There was the ritual of sunning themselves each morning; without fail. Amongst the meerkats who sunned themselves was *Miggy*, the matriarch of *Colony Zero* also called *Miggytown*. There were five such other meerkat colonies. In the morning, most of the meerkats would sun themselves, in clumps of mobs across the valley. Some would later forage in the open spaces and it was striking to see so many sentries posted by the colonies for safety.

Miggy was affectionately called *Mig*. At twelve of age, she was the oldest in the colony. Her alpha-male counterpart was *Densa*. He was old too and had a full set of whiskers. He walked gingerly and was known to be very fast whenever the sentry sounded the alarm. In a way, that is why he had survived for so long.

In *Mig's* mob, one could count twenty-six meerkats. Among them were youngsters. There were a few babies too, the pups. These pups played all day. They would run in the tunnels and around in underground rooms squealing. Each time the alarm sounded, they would follow minders deep into the burrows to safety. They did this several times each day.

The lactating adults looked after the pups. They had no babies, but all the same, looked after *Mig's* pups. During the hot mid-day sun, they laid in the underground rooms. Here they groomed themselves. The most significant pastime was digging deeper into the burrow for food. They found grubs, scorpions and many others which they shared with the pups. Their counterparts, the males, also helped look after the puppies.

Mig was a well-respected elder in the lair. She was feisty and fierce. She liked to wander across the burrows, making sure that everything was in order. They had well-connected tunnels, and *Mig* could walk for several metres underground without having to surface. *Colony Zero* was right in the middle of it all and it had good connections to the other colonies. *Mig* walked deliberately. She often walked around with her hand on her hips.

Abinatu was born six years ago. She had the gift of a leader, and she led *Colony One*. *Nelope* was in charge of *Colony Two*. *Nelope* was nine and domineering. She had the personality and demeanour to match. *Lumos* was mostly quiet but athletic. She had grown her group from three and steadily to thirty-five in *Colony Three*. She was a good mother and would do anything to keep her mob together.

Racie was ruthless, devious with average intelligence. She was also incompetent and quick to anger. Most often, *Racie* felt she was more important than anyone. She was the matriarch of *Colony Four*. *Bello*, on the other hand, was very personable but firm. She controlled *Colony Five*. Her gait was the result of an attack many years ago. *Silentfoot* severely injured her hind legs in two places. The story of the meerkat life followed similar patterns in the *Plain of Plenty*, otherwise known as *Meerdom*.

CHAPTER THREE
EXCITED TO START

Project beginnings are usually exciting, especially for the project manager. The project plan lays out the project objectives, the scope of the project, what is out of scope, related projects, constraints, assumptions, costs, project structure, roles and responsibilities, communications plan, stakeholders, risk management plan amongst several others. To implement the project, the project implementation team has to attack the problem head-on and address issues identified as significant. It usually involves the implementation of new technologies, concepts and ideas. It is often an excellent time to be involved in the project.

The Meerkats in the Plain of Plenty

EXCITEMENT

Mig had been keeping a chart of meerkat populations and had noticed a steady increase of fatalities over the past several seasons. Each mob, except *Colony Four*, had lost on average about four meerkats to the rogue band of hyenas that roamed the *Plain of Plenty*. *Colony Four* lost only one meerkat. The meerkats were also under constant fear of the eagles. These birds appeared to always hover in the sky just waiting for the right time to swoop and take a meerkat. These fatalities, if allowed to rise, would be very catastrophic to the meerkat morale and population.

Before all this, there appeared to be few predators. Food supplies were ample. Meerkats, though all somehow related, had learned to live next door to each other. According to the records *Mig* kept, nasty invaders disturbed the serenity of the plains about ten seasons ago. Meerkats now live an edgy life. Their foraging areas were reduced, and were afraid to wander further out to the extremities of their boundaries for food. This fear led them to clash over food and very soon their situation would be dire. *Mig* was afraid the clashes would become more frequent and a threat to the safety of all meerkats.

The number of colonies had grown either by forceful eviction of siblings or the assemblage of "left-overs" from other communities to form newer colonies. So though they belonged to different colonies, they were from the same lineage.

The five mobs feuded, and this concerned the matriarchs. They have attacked each other over foraging grounds. *Mig* and many of the leaders thought these fights were unnecessary, but they happened anyway. They had all grown weary of the battles, but none of them was in the mood for compromise or peace. It was an uneasy peace.

It troubled *Mig*. These adversaries were her siblings, sons and daughters. She had longed for the day they could talk to each other without the inevitable fights between them. She wanted the past buried because as a bloodline, they all faced extermination by the *Sharp Teeth Gang*.

Mig was old and frail. Her figure showed her age. She

10

despaired about the future of meerkats in the plains. The *Sharp Teeth Gang* had total control of the plains. Amongst them was *Bigjaws*, who had jaws so strong, he could crack through the brain of a juvenile meerkat. Then there was *Hopper* who could bound over shrubs without touching the ground while *Silentfoot*, the leader of the gang, was sly and quick. That is how he earned his name. This gang had even harassed and banished old and lame *Bigbushyhead*, the grumpy old hyena, from his favourite loitering place several hundred metres to the south of *Miggytown*.

In the sky, the eagles ever seemed to hang up there. They would glide on thermals in ever-increasing circles and once so often dive for prey. This diving behaviour frightened the meerkats very much because of its pinpoint accuracy. And there were the drongos too. They kept up with their tricks and annoyingly deprived meerkats of grubs and scorpions.

Life had become a real fight for existence. Meerkat now devoted much of their time to listening out for warning calls from sentries when out in the open. They were unable to forage for much of the day. The pups and juveniles were going hungry, very hungry. Some measures had to be instituted to correct this.

Mig summoned *Adelami*, her trusted confidant and advisor and said to her, "I am old, and I believe that the end is near for me. I feel my age in my bones. I doubt I will see another good harvest season. We may be due for a dry spell with little food, and we will certainly fight over foraging grounds, which is not good for any of us. I am worried about what is going to happen to us. I despair what the future holds if we continue this way. Our colonies must live in peace. And I will tell you this, when there is peace in the country, the chief does not carry a shield. I charge you to organise a meeting with all the matriarchs of the colonies to talk about peace. Use your charm. Flatter them. Make this happen. It is about our very survival. Please. Densa, my companion, will go with you."

Adelami and *Densa* carefully planned the trips and visited all the other five colonies spread over the *Plain of Plenty*. They were given very frosty receptions at *Colonies Two* and *Four*. At *Tallgrass Point*, *Colony Three*, *Lumos* wanted them to stay a few days to see the feast of the mid-day sun. They were verballed at *Colony Two* by three unruly juveniles but for the timely intervention of *Nelope*. Despite these, the force of arguments by *Adelami* and *Densa* prevailed. *Abinatu, Nelope, Lumos, Racie* and *Bello*; the matriarchs of the colonies, agreed to meet with *Mig* at *Miggytown* the next Friday afternoon.

Friday came and all the matriarchs had come to *Colony Zero*. Every matriarch was seated in *The Dome of the Grubs* except *Racie*, having been ushered in by *Adelami*. They waited for the meeting to start with some uneasiness. *Racie* was late for the meeting, and they wondered if *Racie* would turn up at all. "Hmm hmm, my dear sisters and children," *Mig* spoke as she rose to her feet. She abruptly paused and waited. *Mig* had seen the silhouette of *Racie* coming down by the west tunnel with her distinctive gait. *Racie* entered and was escorted by *Adelami* to her seat to sit down.

"You warm my heart with your presence," Mig continued. "I am delighted and thankful you came to hear me. As you can see, I am not what I used to be. I am in the twilight of my life. I do not believe I have many more seasons left in me. I may not be here much longer. Right now I wish to acknowledge every one of you." She paused and gave a wave to Abinatu. She continued, "Good day, *Nelope*. Good day, *Lumos*. Good day, *Racie*. Good day, *Bello* and Good day, *Abinatu*. I hope you are all well. Welcome, and thank you for coming."

She continued, "Frankly, I have had this on my mind for some time. The fatalities we are experiencing is very worrying. My chart shows a significant uptick, and it is not good for us considering our fights and silly rivalries. I dearly want it stopped between our mobs. We have been fighting each other for far too long. I want us to make peace with each other because we are all one blood. What hurts you hurts me." She stopped and wiped a tear. "We have far too many problems confronting us to waste time and resources feuding. We should be above our anger and dislikes. We should expect greater things from ourselves for the sake of those that are yet to come after us."

She paused and stared into their faces. She picked up

again, "One of our biggest problems, to me, is the ever-present *Sharp Teeth Gang*. This gang is a considerable threat to our very existence. The gang has made it difficult for us to live in and grow our colonies without fear. They have taken many a sentry on duty. They have killed many of our men; young and old. We have to push back. We have to protect ourselves at least from the gang. We have to harness the energies we are using to fight each other to fight the *Sharp Teeth Gang* and other predators. We cannot and could not engage them in physical fights, but we should use our intelligence. We have to make it difficult, if not impossible, for the *Sharp Teeth Gang* and other predators to take any of us. We can and should outsmart them. We should find ways to protect ourselves; to protect our mobs. We can do this if we have peace, if we are united and if we work together. Please!"

Mig continued, "Over the past several weeks we have witnessed an increase in the frequency of attacks of the *Sharp Teeth Gang* and other predators. We have lost several juveniles and have seen several members of our mobs from all colonies sustain, sometimes, horrendous injuries in escapes. How long will this continue? How long can we carry on like this? We are under constant attack from the sky and from the bushes too. I have thought long and hard, and I have decided to make a substantial sum available for our protection. I make it available towards the building of fortifications along some of our well-travelled routes, at least. The fortifications should protect us from direct attacks. Please remember peace is costly, but it is worth the expense." As *Mig* sat down, the other matriarchs rose in applause.

Her sincere appeal had touched the matriarchs. There was general chatter amongst them as they conferred with each other. *Abinatu*, who deputised for *Mig*, had previously been put forward as the spokesperson for the group. She liaised with the rest and rose to respond to *Mig*. She queried the matriarchs *"Has any of you anything to say before I address Mig on your behalf?"* They all nodded and signalled in agreement for *Abinatu* to address *Mig*. *Abinatu* began. "Our dear *Mig*. Your concerns touch us, and I believe I speak for all the matriarchs gathered here. Your donation is very welcome

13

and timely too. Peace will be a good thing. With peace, we can achieve a lot."

Abinatu continued, "Rain does not fall on one roof alone. If we succeed, everyone everywhere in the mobs will be safer. We should remember that in a fight, two small antelopes can beat a big one. We can beat these predators. And I have to stress that if we continue to fight like we do now, we only bring joy to the eagle. We mean no comfort for the eagle so we will not fight each other. We will stand united to overcome our problems as alluded to by *Mig*. Tell me this, if relatives help each other, what evil can hurt them?". I believe we will do what is right. We will consult widely in our various colonies and report back here."

The matriarchs agreed to meet the following week to discuss reports from the various colonies and agree on next steps. Before the meeting broke up, *Abinatu* added they should consider the following points in their colony meetings:

- The import of the proposal before them
- Problems, issues, challenges et cetera that they would contend with
- Meerkat resources and material resources that would be required
- Time they had to allocate to this work
- The nature of commitment to this project, and
- Who would fulfil the roles currently undertaken by the project resources?

They were also tasked to deliberate briefly on:

- Belling the leaders of the *Sharp Teeth Gang*
- Building fortifications around the colonies and links between burrows.
- Placing the tunnel entries strategically in the foraging grounds to reduce the chance of ambushes.

A day later, at *Colony Three*, was the day after the big harvest of worms at *Tallgrass Point*. It had rained all day the day before. The ground was wet and soggy. The worms had wiggled out of their burrows and wiggled around in random fashion. They made a sumptuous meal for the *Tallgrass Point* colony.

The rain had eased off earlier in the morning and retreated into the hills. It returned late in the afternoon with much wind and hail. It pelted down, and the sound muffled as they thumped against broad leaves. It was heavy and formed pools of brown water which meandered over the ground invading low ground. It flooded many sections of the tunnels at *Tallgrass Point*.

Lumos watched and was impressed as *Kiikidee*, affectionately called KKD, organised the colony to salvage several sections of the tunnels, save food stores and help the pups and the sick. In the quiet of the afternoon the day after the heavy rains, *Lumos* summoned her colony to discuss *Mig's* proposal. *Lumos* had thought deeply about *Mig's* proposition and its relevance to her colony. The colony had lost sentries, five of them, a week before the rainy season began. Several baby meerkats also did not survive when they were left stranded during frantic runs to tunnels when danger alarms sounded. Even, *Shoobee*, the smart and quick runner, was taken when she tripped over and fell after having saved several baby meerkats. So much fear had gripped the colony.

Lumos addressed the gathering deep in the tunnel. She was deliberate with her choice of words and demeanour. She strove to motivate them to accept that their fate was in their own hands. That it was worth their while to fight back any way they could to ensure their safety. She queried, "What price the life of a baby meerkat? What price the life of a sentry? Each meerkat taken from this colony is one pair of eyes less to look out for you and I! How long are we going to wait until we are all taken? Let us act now. Our very survival as a colony and as Meerdom, in general, is at stake. Let us do this. Let us brainstorm ideas for our protection and survival. I need some good ideas to take to the meeting of matriarchs."

A juvenile suggested they migrated to the lands in the east. *"Why not lead an utterly underground existence?"* asked another. Many such ideas were tossed up for discussion. KKD proposed the building of fortifications around the colonies. He further suggested that gated tunnels linking all colonies would ensure security once they had escaped into their burrows. He elaborated that the reinforcement would be upturned spiked V-shaped structures over the paths to foraging grounds that would enable safe escape from the hyenas.

For the slithering predators, *KKD* enthused that the gates in the tunnels between colonies would enable invaded colony members to escape to nearby tunnels and at the same time shut the gate to stop these slithers pursuing them. *Pimpi*, the joker, suggested that they bell the leaders of the clan of hyenas to loud laughter from the mob. *Lanka* indicated that they agreed to make a regular peace offering to the hyenas to which *Aki* screeched *"And who is going to talk to them? How many of us will be in each offering? And will they even listen to us? This is suicide. This is crazy"*. The discussion of ideas continued for some time yet. The group agreed that the fortification and link tunnel idea was a better one to be sent forth from *Tallgrass Point*. There was joy in the community. There was optimism in the colony. More than two-thirds of the colony put up their paws to take part in the project. Notable among them were *KKD, Kyisa, Vole, Ganya* and *Koobi. Lumos* moved to end the discussions. She announced that she was going to put *KKD* forward for the project manager role before *The Big Six* based on his organisational skills.

Over at *Colony Five*, it had been a tough day of deliberations. The mood was downbeat. *Bello* and her mob had struggled to accept that there was a problem. They felt reasonably secure and did not believe in the *Fortifications* idea. It was going to cost them too much time for, supposedly, a little benefit they said. They had suffered only three fatalities in three seasons.

Bello wanted to be a good corporate citizen. She believed in the general survival of meerkats and argued vigorously for her community to join the project. She wanted to partake in the project despite her misgivings because deep down she knew they had had better luck. The fact was her colony was sheltered among thick bushes and rocky outcrops. Further, the tree stumps also served as high vantage points for their sentries.

Bello discounted the argument that if the rest had put

much effort into nurturing shrubs and strategically placing tunnel openings, they would not have suffered high casualties. *Kismy* and *Dodi* agreed to take part confidently believing that they would play leading roles in the project. Other than that they were very sceptical of the fortifications proposal.

The second Friday came. There was a buzz as *The Big Six* again assembled in *The Dome of the Grubs*. Each matriarch had consulted her colony and had come back with a report of their ideas. *Racie's* mob was not enthusiastic. *Racie* arrived with no proposal insisting she would "go" with whatever was agreed. They have hyenas hunting the grounds next door, but they had them very well covered. They had three sentries watching all the time and also the environs was full of tree stumps.

The meeting of the matriarchs proceeded as agreed. At the gathering *Abinatu*, acting on behalf of *Mig* thundered, *"Today, if we stand tall, it is because of those who have gone before us. It is going to be historical, and I believe we will achieve a lot here today."* There was overwhelming support for the *"Building of fortifications around the colonies and links between burrows"*. The Big Six agreed to call it the *Fortifications Project* and also appointed *KKD* the project manager. *KKD* would report to the matriarchs with *Mig* as the head of *The Big Six*.

Even before the ink on *KKD's* appointment was dry, the need for the project became ever more evident. For it is said, *"A restless feet may walk into a snake pit."* It has been said over and over again but *Ginger*, the ginger-haired meerkat from *Colony Two*, would not listen. It served no purpose screaming at him. He broke with tradition and had put all the mobs at peril. *Ginger* was not supposed to venture on to the plain alone. He was to wait and go out there as a mob with a sentry posted for security of all. Why he did what he did was a mystery to everyone. Four days past he was at it again. He sneaked out during the hot midday sun to gnaw at the roots of the big tree in the foraging bay. He was fortunate to be alive. It appeared he enjoyed life in the fast lane. He took refuge in a bolt hole. For *Ginger* alone, the *Fortification Project* was worth it.

CHAPTER FOUR

FINDING YOUR WAY THROUGH A PROJECT

At the start of projects, project managers are overwhelmed with oodles of documents about the project. These documents, though usually very good, do not tell the whole story of the project. As a project manager, there would be certain facts that you would need to know. There are certain questions that you would only ask, and there would be subtleties, you as the project manager would only pick up. These would usually not be captured well or at all, and you would need to obtain them to understand your project.

One of the illuminating documents a project manager could have is the Project Overview Statement. The project manager, apart from the project brief and other materials, should conduct his own investigation into the "project". During the quick and brief studies, he would learn a lot about the project, for example, the project champions, project haters, how people feel about the project, who to turn to for advice etc. He would learn who actually wants the project to succeed and who paid lip service to the project. The project manager is supposed to know a lot and play the "project management game" according to what he knew, learned, and what came across his table.

The project manager should never go into a project blind, or he is "dead meat". As the project manager, you would be well advised to have your own "knowledgebase" to carry you through the project.

What is happening?
Does anyone know?

* * *

MOVE AHEAD AMIDST CONFUSION

KKD set out to plan and implement the project. But first, he had to cobble together his project team. To achieve buy-in and commitment for the *Fortifications Project*, he produced a *Project Overview Statement* as his first activity in as little time as possible. On the onset, he arranged and interviewed and/or discussed the project with all the matriarchs and the other project champions and opinion leaders. He captured their knowledge and understanding of the project and more importantly, what in their opinion, amongst many others, were:

Reasons for the project - Why was the project being done? Why was the project necessary, and why do it at all?

Project governance and roles - Who was looking after the project? What were the crucial roles for the project?

Objectives of the project - What were the objectives of the project? What were the aims of the project?

Scope of the project - What did the project encompass? What was part of the project? What was not part of the project?

Approach options to the implementation of the project - What were the options available to the project? What made an option sound? Why was that option vital to the implementation of the project?

Expectations - What were the expectations of the project? What did the stakeholders expect to see as the implementation of the project progressed?

His responsibilities and authority as a project manager - What the responsibility of the project manager? Did the project manager have absolute authority on how the project was carried out? Did he have the authority to hire and fire? Was the project manager in full control of the project? Or the project manager had to act at the direction of the leader of *The Big Six*.

Resources that were required and what they were able to contribute to the project - Would the project have first taken on any resources available to run the project? What percentage of the time would be spent on the project? Did the project manager have any say in the allocation of the resources' time?

Important stakeholders - Who were considered important stakeholders? Why were they considered important stakeholders? Were they important because of their role in the project? Were they important because of their size on the project?

Risks, issues, problems, assumptions and constraints - What were the main risks facing the project? What were the show stoppers to the project? What were the main issues in the project? What could be done with the main issues for the project? What were the main problems facing the project? Could the problems be easily addressed? What were the main assumptions? Why was it an assumption? What were the main constraints of the project? What made it a constraint?

Schedule - What was the main driver of the schedule? What was the schedule like? What was likely to affect the schedule?

He compiled the information gathered from the interviews and from available project documentation into a *Project Overview Statement* for distribution and comment by the participants. This approach served several purposes, including:

- His introduction to *The Big Six*, senior management and important stakeholders;
- Quick and deep insight into the organisation and project management culture;
- A greater appreciation of their understanding or misunderstanding of the project, perceived problems, issues, constraints;
- Recognition of project champions and "not-so-enthused" senior executives or opinion leaders;
- Establishment of rapport with participants thus the beginnings of cementing the buying and commitment to the project; and
- The revelation of problems, contradictory positions or information, and misconceptions about the project.

He subsequently developed project plans in consultation with (at least) key stakeholders and senior management regarding the:

- Target audience - these were groups that had to be managed well for the success of the project – e.g. *The Big Six*, project implementation team;
- Key messages - the messages that had to be delivered; not all messages were important for each group – e.g. Key organisational outcomes, risks and significant issues, status and progress etc.
- Communication medium - because of the myriad of communications channels, each group would like to have this presented in a particular way – e.g. in Status Reports, personal briefings, meetings, e-mail, bulletins etc. and
- Frequency of communication - how often and extent of the communication.

On the onset, the *Project Overview Statement* indicated that the matriarch of *Colony 4, Racie,* and her people were not supporters of the project. They saw little return to them. The project's most prominent supporters were *Abinatu* and *Lumos. KKD* had to actively cultivate and solicit their support. He mulled over the document and absorbed what it told him. He assembled the project team from the best people available but yet was sensitive to all talent that was available to him. In the end, he had sixteen people on his team. The talent was:

- A construction engineer
- Four carpenters
- Ten other crew with diverse skills, and
- A quality assurance engineer.

The main chunks of work for the Fortifications Project were:

- To strengthen the entrance of burrows
- To reinforce the gates at the entrance to the burrows
- Cover the tracks to the burrows with inverted V-shaped wooden spikes
- To build communication links and runners between the entries
- To declutter, clean and strengthen the bolt holes in the foraging areas, and lastly
- To create fast and easy access between burrows.

* * *

The project was a considerable undertaking and had a substantial risk. The Issues and Risks Registers were buzzing with entries. The most significant risk was building under constant threat of being taken by predators. They had to counteract this threat, and *KKD* deduced that three sentries at each construction post would mitigate that risk. Yes, the whole project depended on the integrity of the three-person-sentry-system. *KKD* had accumulated a sufficient body of evidence to show that the implementation would be flawless if the three-person-sentry-system worked every time. Once it failed, everything fell apart - any meerkat on the project site could be taken. The most important thing was that, in their escape, no one person hindered another person. It would be catastrophic for the escapees to tumble in one mass and mess for the predator to feast on.

They practised escaping from predators a whole day until they got it right. Occasionally too, he held escape drills to keep them alert. They practised escape to the bolt holes also; and for how long the crew that escaped into the bolt holes stayed. A pilot project was run and evaluated, and after several trials and tweaks, *KKD* decided to build the fortifications beginning with *Colony Three*. *KKD* talked to his project team and discussed every detail in full. The work then started, and it was estimated that the whole construction would go on for eight months.

They made haste slowly and were systematic. It was clear that project implementation team members were living on borrowed time. They had to be on alert every time. There were little room and time to spare. They carried on with the work, and it appeared things were working. However, certain events did not go so well, and things started to turn badly.

They seemed to lurch from one crisis to the next. The crises were traced to flaws in *Kismy* and *Dodi's* work. Their commitment was very suspect, and in several instances, they did shoddy jobs. It was found that the rail wheel did not align with the rail tracks. The implementation team had to rework and clean up the work.

Two days later, it was a test day for the tensile strength in the back wall of burrow anchors. Unexpectedly, the sentries barked and every meerkat run to refuge in the burrows. *KKD* was last to escape and could not shut the gate after him. The shutting mechanism failed.

After the danger had passed, the failure of the shutting mechanism was analysed. It was determined that the latch was ten millimetres short and thus was unable to be hooked on the wall. It took the implementation team four days to rework the whole mechanism.

A pattern started to emerge, so *KKD* called a meeting of the project team. Analysis of the mishaps pointed to intervention by some of the workers. The trail led to *Kismy* and *Dodi*. *KKD* was furious and confronted them. They, of course, denied working as saboteurs on the project.

The project was working to a really tight schedule with some firm deadlines. *KKD* demanded of *The Big Six* that *Kismy* and *Dodi* be taken off the project team. They had committed grievous acts that could have led to fatal consequences. *KKD* demanded he had a hand in *Kismy* and *Dodi's* replacements; both came from the same *Colony Four* though.

The replacements were done, but things were not the same again. They were suspicious of wreckers, and *KKD* and other senior project members spent considerable capital and expense checking and cross-checking their calculations, the cutting of wood, the assemblages and rail tracks in particular. This took its toll and made a difficult job more tedious. It became boring and disillusionment set in.

CHAPTER FIVE

TIME TO CATCH THE CULPRITS

Projects are small organisations. As the project manager, you have the responsibility of making sure that every aspect works. You are the leader, and you have to take responsibility for all that goes on in the project. Some times projects tick and everything works fine.

On specific projects, you might have the luxury of picking your resources. God bless you if that happens. But in the real world, you have none of these rights. You take what you are giving, and you are expected to work with the team. You might try very hard to work with several individuals, but in all likelihood, there would be people who would not play ball with you.

Many of these resources come from positions of power in the organisation and like to exercise that power. Some would kick back against whatever you do. They would want transference of their power base to the project. They would see you as a usurper of their power. They would never accept you, but you have to find a way to work with them. However, many would do the right thing and would work with you.

You have to mould the many characters into a working machine to deliver the project. It would be in the delivery of the project that the human aspects came out. Their friendships, their managerial responsibilities, supervisory roles, critical lines of authority would, among several factors, would overwhelm many of them and tip the project into trouble. You would have to find the troublemakers and set them right; one way or the other. It always happens. It is a fact of life. If you did not, your hold on the project is doomed.

Time to catch the culprits

It wasn't me

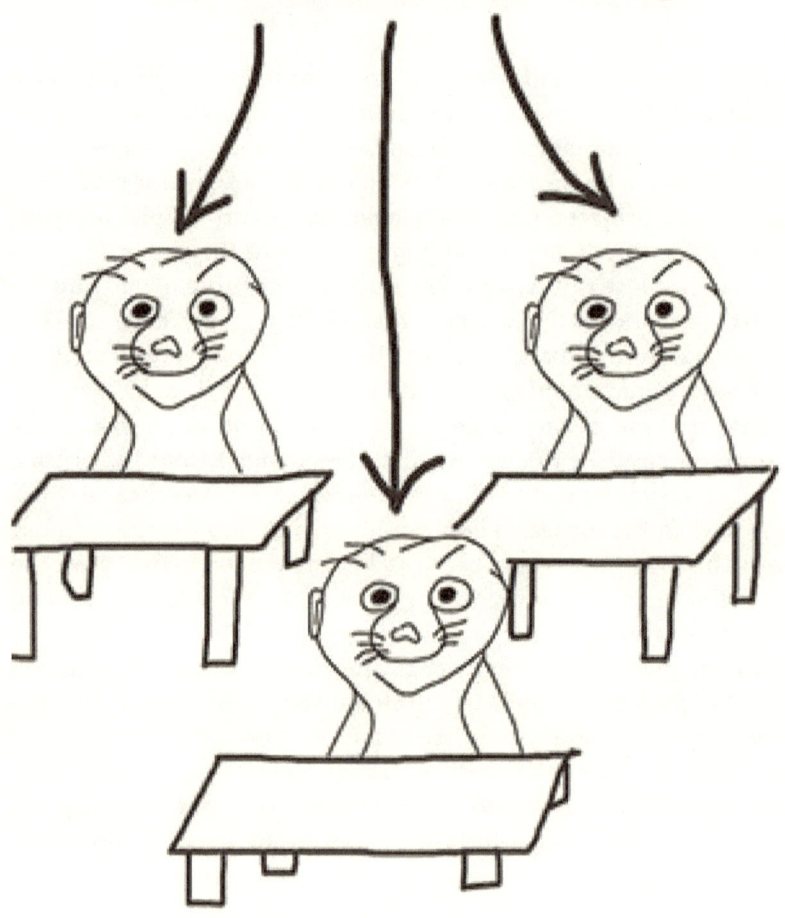

GET THE WRONG DOERS

Kismy and *Dodi* did not go quietly. They charged that *KKD* and the rest of the project team were provoking knee-jerk responses. They said they had been denied natural justice and procedural fairness. They charged that what *KKD* and the project team had concocted was a solution looking for a problem to solve. And that it might lead to undesired outcomes.

Meanwhile, there was trouble in the project management team. *Nita*, who was the construction engineer, had easy access to *Racie*, one of *The Big Six*. She spent several hours in *Racie's* office, supposedly walking *Racie* through construction matters. *Nita* was also, at the same time, a life long friend of *Racie*. *Nita* thus had an undue influence on the project to the chagrin of the *KKD*.

Nita, though, had not shown it, did not like *KKD*. *KKD* made her uneasy and asked her direct probing questions regarding her work like the project manager should. *Nita* believed *KKD* did not value her contribution to the project as a whole. She, therefore, held back and did not share openly with the rest of the implementation team. On *KKD's* calculations, *Nita* was supposed to have completed most of her drawings for the fortifications. All the wood was supposed to have been cut to specifications too.

Nita, through her work, got to know what each one did and somehow inserted herself into their project tasks. *Nita* interfered with the scheduling of tasks. *KKD* came to realise that *Nita* was virtually making subtle changes to the schedule. It was unfortunate that *Mig* could not fulfil her role as leader of *The Big Six* as *KKD* could not obtain sympathetic hearing from the other *Big Six*. These matriarchs, haven seen *Racie* forcefully fill the role of de facto leader, deferred responsibility of the project to *Racie* too. They did not want to make an issue about project leadership. Getting *Racie* involved in the project was "good enough" than have her work against the project from the outside.

All *KKD* wanted to do was an approach that when implemented was proven and worked. Unfortunately for

KKD, *Kismy* and *Dodi* were also in league with *Nita*, and it was clear that the project manager had not known about it. This turned out to be a very fatal mistake in the scheme of things. The project was at a critical stage, and *KKD* had to expend most of his time managing several aspects of the project. *KKD* hoped things will work out as the days went along.

Three days later, *KKD* had a top-secret arrangement to test one theory. It was postulated that the the survival of meerkats was greatly enhanced on *application of strong scent-mark on subordinates* before encampment in bolt holes. He had canvassed this test with *The Big Six* and *Bello*, the matriarch of *Colony 5* and her alpha-male counterpart, *Zinzi*, who had agreed to participate.

There was secrecy surrounding this activity and justifiably so. There was a clear and distinct possibility of mass casualties should things go terribly wrong and they were attacked before they escaped into the bolt hole. This test was to cover the extremes of the boundaries of *Colonies Five* and *Zero*. It was to be done at about 10:30 in the morning when the weather was not too hot. This was also after the meerkats have had breakfast.

Two days before testing the theory, the implementation team had prepared the grounds setting up the sentry posts. There were three sentry posts about a hundred metres apart. Six bolt holes had all been decluttered, patched up and strengthened. On the morning of the test, *Bello* and *Zinzi* applied fresh scent-marks to the sixteen volunteers.

The team then advanced cautiously from one post to the next. On the alarm, scent-marked meerkats escaped into the bolt-holes for as long as the danger prevailed. It was a long day, and at the end of it, it appeared *KKD* had proven the scent-marks appeared worked. So either the scent-marks repelled the predators, or some other mechanism was at work. For *KKD*, just knowing that everything went well was more than he wished for.

CHAPTER SIX

JUST PERSECUTE ANYONE

A project manager has a target painted on his or her back. The project manager is so involved in the running of the project that he or she invariably forgets other games people play. He needs to have good people around him. He needs to watch his back. If he did not have the right team, someone would jump out of the left field and wipe him out.

People jostle for the role of project manager, especially after the project manager had done the hard work of putting the project on a solid footing. In those times, the project manager might fall with the "culprits" that the system threw up. In those dark hours, he would wonder what happened to him. He would wonder how someone, almost invariably, in his close circle, would pull the rug from under his feet? How come the project champion abandoned him on the altar of expediency? But once support is lost, there is only one action left to take - quit. Remember, project managers also die.

Now it was all in the open. *KKD* had been brought down. *Nita* was a big part of the coup, and they had to take control of the project now. There were misgivings in the project implementation team that had to be addressed. *Racie* and *Nita* had to act fast to stop the rot. In a way, *KKD* made it so easy for them. All the blueprints were available, and it was a case of "rinse and repeat". The rest of the project implementation team either had to fall in with *Nita* or step down. Many did, but others continued.

HOUND THOSE THAT DID RIGHT

Now there was additional fortification test to be done. The quality assurance engineer, *Miko,* had to ensure that the structures were sound and robust. He had a team of four working with him to test the rigidity of the fittings. They tested each and every single link in the chain. The group agreed to carry out a dry acceptance test since they had to ensure that nothing broke. The acceptance test had been done for *Colonies Two, Three* and *Four.* It was just a matter of carefully following the laid down and tested procedural steps. It was, however, vital the dry run was done to ensure everything worked as planned.

The dry acceptance test was arranged and scheduled for *Colony Five.* On the morning of the dry acceptance test, *Nita* convinced *Racie* to conduct a live acceptance test instead to save four days of work. *KKD* had earlier decreed that each acceptance test would first have a dry run. He wanted to ensure that he went through the steps one-at-a-time to ensure they worked. He wanted to be able to, like before, determine where things went wrong. He wanted to catch all the steps and record them for later for the project library.

KKD was in a meeting with *Mig* briefing her on the bolt hole testing while *Miko* undertook the acceptance test! *Nita*, through *Racie*, had her way and ran the acceptance test live. They hit some snags and tried to rectify the situation. The latch mechanism to several locks had failed to fire. These snowballed and resulted in a catastrophic failure.

It was a test that should have been done as a dry run. It did not need to be run live. When it failed, *Nita* and *Racie* stated that they followed the procedure *KKD* put in place. Before *KKD* could refute that and sanction *Nita*, *Racie* controversially sacked *KKD*. *Racie* did not want the rest of the project team and the rest of all *Meerdom* to know the truth. *Racie* was uncomfortable with the truth and wanted it buried with *KKD's* sacking. KKD was terminated immediately and on the spot.

KKD and his team had laboured for so long to build the fortifications. They had built the fortifications for *Colonies Two*, *Three* and *Four*. It was clear that the fortifications were fit for purpose, and it was beginning to save lives. Only one meerkat had been killed since the fortifications were built. *KKD* relied on his project management skills, and he did not kowtow to anyone. He believed the quality of his work would shield him and so did not cultivate any patronage by senior officers in the organisation. It was not his nature to let top management cover for his mistakes. He had always been that way. *Nita*, on the other hand, hid under the coverage of *Racie*. *Racie* covered for *Nita*, and they got rid of *KKD*.

KKD lost his job, and all in the project implementation team knew their jobs were on the line too. There was a new king, and that meant a new broom to sweep the cupboard clean. Anyone that was closely aligned with *KKD* either had to go or toe the line. The hounding of the innocents had begun and continued through the project. Many members of the implementation team, anyone that had a conscience, had to walk. They either resigned or were forced out. It was said their personalities did not fit in and had to be replaced.

The project work continued despite the hounding. The fortifications were built to cover *Colonies Zero, One* and *Five*. The work had been fabricated, and all they had to do was replicate the assembling of it. It was repetitive but had to be watched closely to ensure success. The blueprints left by *KKD* was of enormous help, and in no time *Meerdom* had built the fortifications against its predators.

CHAPTER SEVEN

REWARD THOSE LEFT STANDING

One of the most rewarding times is at project handover. You, as the project manager, have managed to steer your project through storm waters, mischievous and calculating individuals to project delivery. At project delivery, everyone is a winner. Everyone worked hard for the project, and all of the characters come out for their fifteen minutes of fame. At handover, each deserved an award; the highest ever possible.

So, the project had been successfully implemented. The entrance of all burrows had been strengthened. The gates at the tunnels had been reinforced, making them more robust. The V-shaped wooden spikes had been carefully laid. The communication links and runners between entrances were also set up. The temporary hideout area, the bolt holes in the open foraging areas had been decluttered and strengthened, and there was fast and easy access between burrows.

The benefits of the project were being realised. Only two meerkats had been taken in the past several weeks. The workers had to be acknowledged and thanked. The awards went to those left standing at the end of the day.

The Decorations

ADORNMENT OF THE OBSERVERS

The project continued to completion. It was apparent that the project had achieved its aim. The benefits were there for everyone to see and acknowledge. Only two meerkats had been taken by predators. The mobs had a more relaxed atmosphere for daily activities. But the sentries still had to be posted. The pups had to be watched. Every meerkat knew that. The changes, in no way, meant the abandonment of common sense. What had changed was the predators could not charge in or dive-bomb the mob and swoop them away.

The last gate was fortified and closed with much fanfare. *The Big Six*, including *Mig*, attended the ceremony. The project implementation team was congratulated for a magnificent build. The following awards were given to the "deserving" members:

The Commendation for Superior Performance on the job - given to all the members of the group of meerkats that provided various services during the implementation of the project.

The Bronze Award to the Watch Group, the group of meerkats that provided sentry services during the implementation of the project.

The Silver Shield Award - awarded to The Construction Manager, for her enormous contribution to the project. It was given to *Nita*.

The Golden Arm of the Sword - awarded to the leader of the project implementation team, the interim project manager. She was commended for her *"excellent management"* of the team and especially during the upheavals that nearly derailed the project. This too went to *Nita*.

The observers had to be congratulated too. They have stood the test of time. They witnessed everything from the start, through the crises and right to the end. They had a story to tell. **One thing was the "heroes" of the project were to remain unsung. That is what it has always been, and that is what it will always be.**

CHAPTER EIGHT
PROJECT COMPLETED!

It has been a long road. The journey from concept to implementation took a terrible toll on the project manager. The project manager fought on his record and lost. He was outwitted and tossed out; blamed for everything and vilified. This has and would always be the course of projects from:

- Enthused to start
- Confusion and worry
- Time to catch the culprits
- Just persecute anyone
- Reward those left standing, and
- Project completed!

So what next?

Useful Resources

Visit https://ditec.com.au/meerdom for news and information on the *Meerdom*.

Ask for a review

I will love to read your reviews of this book. One of the ways that you can bless me as a writer is by writing an honest and candid review of this book on Amazon.

To write to me about this book or to share any other thoughts, please feel free to contact me at this address meerdom@ditec.com.au

www.ingramcontent.com/pod-product-compliance
Lightning Source LLC
Chambersburg PA
CBHW030539220526
45463CB00007B/2907